50p
1/25

The
SPUR BOOK
of
WINTER CAMPING

Other titles in
SPUR VENTURE GUIDE
SERIES include:

Unless otherwise listed, by Brown & Hunter

Spur Footpath Guides include:

Send for a full list of titles

The
SPUR BOOK
of
WINTER CAMPING

Rob Hunter and Terry Brown

SPURBOOKS LIMITED

Published by
SPURBOOKS LTD.
6 Parade Court
Bourne End
Bucks

ISBN 0 904978 78 8

Printed by Maund & Irvine, Ltd. Tring, Herts.

CONTENTS

PUBLISHER'S INTRODUCTION

ABOUT THIS SERIES

Venture Guides fall into two broad areas. The first group aims to provide the outdoor enthusiast with a range of those outdoor skills which every outdoor activity involves. They therefore cover knot-tying, map and compass work, weather lore, first aid, camping skills and survival techniques, chart work, and outdoor cookery.

The second group covers Venture sports such as dinghy sailing, canoeing, rock climbing, ski-ing, snorkelling, cross country ski-ing, hill-trekking and backpacking.

A full list of Venture Guides will be found in the title pages of this book, and they can be obtained from all good bookshops or outdoor equipment suppliers.

ABOUT THIS BOOK

Until quite recently, anyone who went camping in the winter met with stares, and the occasional jeer. "You must be mad" was the kindest comment. In the last few years though, all this has changed, and people are now camping all through the year, and increasingly in winter. The backpacking season for example, a growing side of the sport, really only starts in October.

Winter camping has many advantages, and the first and greatest is that it revives camping as it used to be, and as it is supposed to be. Gone are the summer crowds, the litter and the noise, the transistors and the football thudding against the tent wall. It's cold, and wet, and a bit rugged, and dammed good fun!

Moreover, winter camping requires technique. In recent years, equipment has all too often replaced technique. You no longer stay on the lee side, out of the wind, you put on your super wondertwill zoot-suit, and plough on through the gale. In the winter that isn't good enough. In winter the balance favours the elements, and you have to use fieldcraft and all sorts of skills, to stay warm, dry and comfortable. Such techniques are the subject of this book.

In our first book in this series, called simply *'Camping'*, we took as our basic party, two people, 'me and my pal', aiming neither at the solitary backpacker or the frame-tent family group. In this one, we will retain our basic unit of two, and assume that we are going on foot. In practice we usually go by car to our starting point, and hump the gear from there, but we will recommend nothing that cannot be packed and carried by two people. We also assume that you have some experience of summer camping, and a good grasp of camping terms.

Chapter 1

WHERE AND WHEN TO GO

The winter camping season starts in October and goes on until
the end of March. During this period, the weather is so
changeable and generally foul, that in spite of mild spells and
moving your camping sites South, you will still need to gear
yourself up for winter conditions.

WHERE TO GO

The first snag is that in winter many camp sites are shut,
although here and there summer sites are starting to stay open in
the winter too. The New Forest has winter sites, and the Forestry
Commission generally seems aware of the growth of winter
camping and are opening more sites throughout the year.
Camping among (not under) trees, is very good in the winter.

The Peak District, the Black Mountains, and the Lake District all
have year-round sites, though obviously far fewer than in the
summer time. On the other hand there are fewer campers, so
that if the site is open you can usually get a pitch.

Try and find a site with showers, or at least some hot water
available. Funnily enough, finding water is often a real problem in
winter. Overall, it's fair to say that there are some year-round
camp sites open in all areas. You can find them in the usual camp
site guides, and in the lists published in magazines like 'Camping'
and 'Practical Camper'.

Winter camping is particularly the province of the backpacker.
(It's all that solitude, you know!) Would-be winter campers or
backpackers should join the Backpackers Club, 20 St Michael's
Road, Tilehurst, Reading, Berkshire.

In winter it is a good idea to link up with some organization like
the Backpackers, and even more essential than in summer to pre-
plan your trip. In remote areas, cafes, hotels, and even shops and
pubs can be shut. Streams can be frozen, standpipes and taps
turned off lest they burst. We know a couple who set off,
moderately equipped, to walk the South Downs Way in
November; it's like the M1 in summer time! When they came
back their story sounded rather like a trek across Siberia. No
shops, no water, dark, shuttered villages, and although they
intended to camp a bit, and stay in guest houses a bit, when the
weather was wet or *they* were, they found that nowhere was
open and they had to stay out all the time. Terrible for them, but
good for us, as their experience added to ours will enhance the
value of this book.

WHEN TO GO

The winter season lasts from October to Easter. This period can encompass some very bad weather, especially on high ground, so hill camping in North Wales, Scotland, the Black Mountains, or anywhere remote over 1000 ft. should not be attempted unless:—

1. You have a companion.

2. You are properly equipped.

3. You have a good weather forecast for the intended trip, *plus one day*.

4. You have the experience.

If the weather promises to be really foul, don't go up the mountain. What are you trying to prove? You can have just as much fun somewhere less hazardous, and perhaps cause less trouble for your friends and the rescue people.

GO SOUTH, YOUNG MAN

You can camp quite happily in winter by camping lower down the mountain, or further South than in summer. Why not move your camping activities to warmer climes? To the South-West, rather than the Lake District. Study a relief map and you can spot suitably rugged areas in the Midlands, Kent, Sussex, or the West Country, uncrowded in winter and worth inspection. Southern footpaths like the Ridgeway, the South Downs Way, or the Cotswold Way, are all worth a winter trip.

Motorways link up the country very well nowadays, so for a start anyway—until you are experienced in winter camping— why not look South.

CAR CARE

This section comes as the result of a plea from the *'management'*. When you leave the car in the winter, spread some newspapers in the boot and on the floor, and put a pair of clean shoes in your car. You will usually return with muddy boots, and often with wet gear. Smearing mud over the family transport makes one very unpopular. So change the boots before driving off. A dry change of clothing in the boot isn't a bad idea either. Be sure the battery has a good charge and spread a newspaper or old blanket over the engine, under the bonnet. This will aid starting after days in the open, but don't forget to remove it before you start up.

SAFETY

You need to take more care in winter, wherever you go. A heavy cold, a bad chill, or a wrenched ankle may not be serious, but it's not much fun either.

This book is not *specifically* designed for those who trek in the hills, but since you may want to, or because many lowland sites are shut it may seem necessary, let us remind you about SAFETY, and let us get the basics right:

1. Never go into the hills on your own.

2. Always leave a route card with some responsible person.

3. Always go properly equipped, with First Aid and Survival equipment.

4. Be sure you are competent in camping and map reading skills, especially at night, and in fog or poor visibility.

5. Be careful on narrow roads in the dark and mist. Walk facing the traffic and have a strip of 'Scotch-lite' reflective tape on your arm or rucksack.

6. Always strain every effort to be dry, fed and sheltered—at least at night.

Carry out these points, as a drill or routine EVERY TIME, not just when on some long trek to, say, the Western Highlands.

THE COUNTRY CODE

We make considerable reference in the course of this book to plastic bags and newspapers. They are *very* useful, but they are not environmental. Never leave plastic bags in the countryside. Cows love 'em, but can and do die from eating them, so take them, and your other rubbish, home. Remember also to shut gates, keep off crops, and ploughed fields. Don't clamber over dry-stone walls, and in every case respect and obey the Country Code.

SUMMER SCALE

We are assuming that you have summer camping experience and kit. Since much of our advice is based on additions to, or alternatives from, this basic summer scale, we are going to list here what we feel the basic two-man *summer* camping kit might consist of. You can add to or subtract from it as you wish. We only suggest it as a yardstick.

Item	Weight
Tent x 1 (including flysheet)	8 lbs
Sleeping bag x 2	6 lbs 4 ozs
Lilo mat or pad x 2	6 lbs 12 ozs
Rucksack/backpack x 2	5 lbs
Stoves x 2 (Paraffin or petrol, Optimus, or Gaz)	3 lbs 8 ozs
Water bottles (plastic, empty)	5 ozs
Cooking gear x 1 (aluminium)	1 lb 4 ozs
Eating gear x 2 (plastic where possible)	1 lb
Torch x 2	1 lb 8 ozs
Spare clothes/track suits—socks, sweater, underwear x 2	8 lbs
Spare shoes, gym shoes x 2	3 lbs
Washing/shaving etc. x 1	1 lb
Survival: space blanket/first aid kit x 1	1 lb
Survival food x 2	2 lbs
For two people =	48 lbs 9 ozs

Note the weight, about 25 lbs each, plus food.

For winter camping you don't necessarily need more gear—with a few exceptions—so much as *different* gear, different weight, material or specification. The amount of *extra* gear is quite small.

Let us now look at ways of supplementing or upgrading this summer kit to make it more suitable for *winter* camping.

HOOD WITH
WIRED VISOR

JACKET WITH ZIP
AND VELCRO FASTENING

OVERTROUSERS
WITH LEG ZIPS

KNEE LENGTH GAITERS

Chapter 2

SUPPLEMENTARY WINTER KIT

It is, we think, a fair assumption that most people will start their camping career in the summer, and purchase gear suitable for the milder weather of spring, summer and early autumn. Since camping equipment is expensive, most people will want to supplement their existing equipment, rather than purchase a completely new set of winter camping gear.

BOOTS

Your usual boots will probably do, but you will need to give the leather a light coating of Kiwi wet-prufe, to aid waterproofing. Cleated, rubber-soled boots are unsafe on ice, frozen grass, mud or wet rock, so be careful. A few tricouni nails screwed into the soles will improve your footing considerably. Don't let the boot heels get smooth, as this can cause slips. Shoes are not adequate in the winter.

GAITERS

A good pair of gaiters is essential in the winter. Buy long ones for winter rather than the short 'stop-tous'.

SOCKS

Wet feet are a great possibility, so carry at least three pairs of extra long socks. If your feet get wet, change your socks. Wet feet are miserable, and wet socks will soften the skin on the feet, and lead to blisters.

OVER-TROUSERS

Waterproof over-trousers are a *must* in the winter. Buy the type with leg gussets or zips, so that you can get them on or off easily, over your boots. You won't want to wear streaming-wet over-trousers in a tent, and if you can slip them off easily, life gets simpler.

WATERPROOF MITTS AND GLOVES

If it's cold, you will want to wear gloves anyway, but a pair of waterproof over-mitts will keep the gloves dry. Put the mitts on a long piece of tape and run this down your sleeves—like Mum does for a small child. Then, you can, if necessary, remove the mitts, stuff the gloves inside them while you are working, thereby keeping the gloves dry and easy to find.

We have used 'danglers' for years, and find them very useful.

HEAVY CAGOULES

Your summer cagoule will probably be too light. You can buy heavy-duty cagoules and they are well worth the money, for you can use them in the summer as well.

TENTS

Unless you have a mountain tent anyway, you must have a tent with a *flysheet,* and the flysheet should have a *porch*.

A flysheet will keep the rain out, help the inhabitants to stay warm, and reduce condensation. The flysheet should reach down to ground level, and be well stitched and guyed.

The flysheet porch will be invaluable as a cooking space, when the weather is nasty. Only in extreme cases should you cook in the tent—and even then only certain foods. (See Chapter 7).

SLEEPING BAGS

A summer bag on its own won't do. You can supplement it with one (or two) inners, with a blanket, or by wearing extra clothing when turning in for the night. It is very important to improve the insulation between the bag and the ground. We'll talk at length about bags later. (See Chapter 4).

MATS OR AIR BEDS?

In our opinion mats are better than air beds in winter. The air in the bed is chilled by the cold ground, and you are, in effect, sleeping on an envelope of cold air. So, if you have an air bed you need:—

1. To insulate the bed from the ground.
2. To insulate the sleeper from the bed.

STOVES

Depending on which stove you have, it will probably do, but it really depends on the fuel. Let's look at fuels separately.

Gas: In the UK most gas cylinders contain butane, which will not gasify at temperatures below zero. Moreover it gets very sluggish at the lower temperatures even above zero, and so cooking times increase. Some stoves have ways of getting round this problem by pre-heating the liquid, but as a general rule gas is not ideal for winter camping, although, this apart, it has other advantages — very clean, light, etc.

If you do have a gas stove you will need to keep the cylinders warm—even having them in your sleeping bag at night. Resign yourself to long waits at mealtimes.

Petrol: Petrol is fine, but you will almost certainly have to cook in the porch or in the tent at some time, and we are not keen on petrol inside tents. If you are *very* careful though, it is excellent, and your petrol stove will do. *Never* fill a stove inside the tent.

Solid Fuel: Solid fuel has many advantages in winter. It is impervious to damp, is light in weight—and you need to save ounces where you can—**and if you ventilate well, and watch the fumes, it is perfectly safe in a tent.**

Paraffin: We think Paraffin is the best in winter. It is comparatively inert. It burns well, and, although paraffin stoves need priming, you can do this with Meta solid-fuel tablets, which are light and avoid the necessity for carrying meths as a primer.

It is important, wherever possible, to avoid carrying two sorts of fuel. If your cooker *and* lamp run on paraffin, you only need one sort, which is weight saving and safer. We dread the thought of people pouring petrol into a hurricane lamp!

Stove Windshields: Even if you don't use them in summer, you will need them in winter. The wind isn't just blowing, it's cold!

Your stove should have a wind-screen, and if it hasn't, you can use a *small asbestos blanket.* Drape this over the stove and cooking pot on the windward side, to keep the wind blowing the flame about.

SAFETY KIT

If you carry the summer scale of plastic bag, space blanket, plastic **survival bag or sheet, chocolate and whistle, you must** *add* **a tent,** a sleeping bag, a stove and some high calorie food, to be equally secure in winter.

RUCKSACK

Your summer sack will probably do and if it is not proofed nylon, you can cover it with a big plastic bag, worn mouth down and sealed with a rubber band, which, although a little un-handy, will keep the rain out.

PLASTIC BAGS

Damp, rain, mud, are the enemies in winter. Take lots of plastic bags in various sizes. They are very useful, but don't leave them behind for cattle to eat.

CLOTHING

The wind is the problem. If you are active, or out of the wind, you will get along quite well with just an extra sweater, and a hat; especially the hat, which you need to keep the head and ears warm.

A track suit, lots of sweaters, wool tights or even pyjamas, can help keep you snug. We'll discuss winter clothing properly in the next chapter.

So let us now list the *extra kit* necessary to upgrade your summer scale for winter use.

You need:—

Clothing:

Sweaters

Woolly hat

Track suit/wool pyjamas

Gaiters

Over-trousers

Heavyweight cagoule

Waterproof mittens

Gloves

Kit:

Flysheet—with porch

Blanket/bag inner

Mat or airbed, with extra insulation

Windshielded stove (Paraffin if possible)

Extra survival kit and rations

16

If you have this, plus your summer scale, you can be warm, fed and dry, in all but the worst weather, in normal lowland conditions. We'll talk about mountain kit later.

WHAT DOES IT COST AND WEIGH?

Since the object of the exercises is to improve the usage of your gear at minimum cost, how much it is going to cost is a relevant question, and the weight is always a problem to foot-borne campers.

We can only give some estimates, but by costing and weighing our *own* gear, we can give you maximums, over and above the summer scale (25 lbs).

Extra weight (maximum)—17 lbs per person.

This *assumes* that your tent does not already have a flysheet, that you don't *already* carry a track suit. You may carry much of this gear already, so the extra weight is not necessarily so much, but it is fair to say that in winter you must expect to carry a weight nearer 40 lbs than 30 lbs.

COST

This is not excessive. Long gaiters cost about £6.00. Over-trousers are about the same. Cagoules from £8.00–£14.00. Many items, blankets, extra food, insulating materials and so on, can be scrounged from around the house, and we feel that a maximum extra cost of around £50.00 will equip you for the winter, and you can probably spend much less.

USAGE

This may, at first sight, seem a fair amount of cash, but remember that it increases the usage of all your gear. If you can camp for the whole 12 months of the year, instead of about 6 months, the extra benefit will more than compensate for the extra cost, and winter camping is more fun, so the enjoyment factor goes up as well! All camping gear increases in price yearly, so it pays to get the maximum use from it.

Chapter 3

WINTER GEAR

Perhaps you are one of those lucky people who can afford special gear for all occasions or maybe you intend to camp all the year round and want to buy all-weather gear to begin with. Given that we had known *then* what we know *now*, this is what we would have done. Remember that, with very few exceptions, you can use more winter gear in the summer, than you can use summer gear in the winter. So, let us equip you, from scratch, for year-round camping.

CLOTHING
From the feet up: Cleated boots, gaiters, stout cord trousers or breeches, with a double seat, wool shirts, string vest and cotton underwear, several sweaters, anorak, hat and gloves.

This is a basic outfit, and with the possible exception of cord breeches and gloves, this is not much different from the normal summer gear. Remember to keep it clean as this helps your clothing retain the warmth-giving qualities.

There are, however, several fairly critical decisions.

ANORAKS AND DUVET JACKETS
Anoraks usually have thin linings, while the best quality duvet jackets are filled with duck-down—or they used to be. It is undeniable that down-jackets are light, warm, and very comfortable. That's the good point. They are also expensive, and become pretty useless if they get wet.

Duvets filled with P2 or Fibrefill 2 synthetic, have the great advantage that they keep thier heat retention qualities even when wet. They are also cheaper than down, and the only real snag is that they are bulkier.

On balance then, buy man-made fibres (Dacron Fibrefill for example) for your all-the-year duvet or anorak.

LONG SOCKS
You can wear "comb's", or a pair of pyjama trousers as extra underwear, if it's really chilly. For normal use, all year round, buy long, knee-length socks. Spare socks are essential in winter.

TROUSERS
Provided you don't wear jeans, which are useless in the wet, and not much protection at any time; any form of wool trousers is fine

for normal use. However, in the winter, cord or tweed breeches are best. Worn with long socks and long gaiters, you don't have wet, chilly bottoms flapping round your ankles. You can't keep loose bottoms dry in winter, for even if the sky is dry, the grass is wet. This is where gaiters come in.

Buy breeches, with a double seat. They stand the wear better, and keep the rear warm when sitting on some frozen rock. Wear a belt *and* braces to keep them up.

SHIRTS AND SWEATERS

The secret of warmth is *layer clothing* and natural fibres like wool. The layers trap dry air and this insulates you from the winter wind.

You will see stalwarts wrapped up in thick oiled wool gear, but we reckon this to be very cumbersome. Fibre-pile zip jackets *(Insulata)* are very cozy for wearing in the tent, or pottering about the site. Make sure shirts and sweaters are long enough not to leave gaps when you bend over.

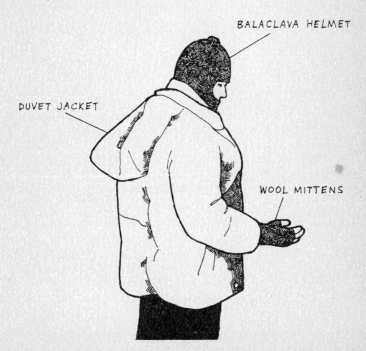

BALACLAVA HELMET

DUVET JACKET

WOOL MITTENS

BOOTS

For year-round camping, it has to be boots. Shoes are not adequate in winter. Most people wear those with the cleated, Vibram or commando-pattern sole. The only snag is that in winter, on ice, wet grass, or mud, rubber soles can slip. The grip can be much improved by having a few climbing nails or tri-counis screwed into the heel and instep. You should really wear nailed boots. The cold can strike up through the sole, so a second pair of thin wool or cotton socks, or an insole, is useful.

CRAMPONS

Crampons are spiked metal "feet", which are strapped on to the boots to provide grip on ice or frozen snow. If you plan on camping in the hills you should have a pair to go with your cleated-soled boots, when crossing ice slopes. They have to be carefully fitted or they will work loose.

GAITERS

Long gaiters are essential for keeping feet and legs dry, and you can take one off to sit or eat from, during a halt.

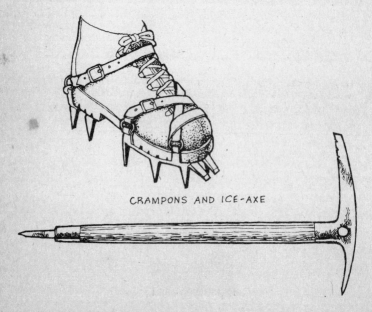

CRAMPONS AND ICE-AXE

WALKING STICK: ICE AXE

There was a time when everyone carried a walking stick—a stick for walking. In the winter a stout stick or ash plant is very handy. Your footholds are less secure than in summer, and you will feel (and be) much safer with a stick. For edging down hillsides, hopping over mud, or testing the depth of puddles before you go squelching in, they are invaluable. Buy one today. However, if you are *intending* to go into the hills, or on snow, then you must have an ice-axe, and know how to brake with it should you slip.

GLOVES AND OVER-MITTS

Wool gloves and nylon windproof mitts are essential. If your hands are frozen it is very difficult to do anything, even to concentrate. Keep the hands, head and feet warm and you'll be happy.

HEADGEAR

Whatever headgear you buy, it must keep the ears covered, or have the potential to do so. A balaclava is fine, but your breath will make it wet around the mouth, and we find them itchy. A wool ski-cap or a beret with a scarf round the ears, will do quite well.

RAIN GEAR—SHELL CLOTHING: PONCHOS

For complete protection for man and rucksack, the poncho has a lot to recommend it. The *Pakjac* is a popular make, comes in a variety of colours and weighs only 11 ozs. It can also be used as a survival bag.

CAGOULE

For year-round and winter use, buy a heavyweight cagoule, not a light one. The stiffer fabric will help keep the wind from beating the chill into you. Check that zips have flaps. If not, the rain can beat through, and snow or ice freeze the zip. Pockets need flaps; a pocket full of rainwater is nasty. It must have a hood, and one with a face opening stiffened with wire is best. You want cuffed sleeves or water will run up your arms.

Ventilation is important with all shell-clothing, as you can get wet from condensation and sweat building up inside. A full-length zip is best for this reason.

OVER-TROUSERS

Most summer campers don't bother with over-trousers. Winter campers will have to, so get the standard or heavy duty type. The 'heavy' doesn't mean they weigh more—or not much more—just that the material is less flimsy.

NIGHTWEAR

As a general rule, it's best to take off as much as possible before turning into the sleeping bag, but in winter this is not always possible. Unless your sleeping bag is completely adequate, you will probably find it necessary to change into some form of sleeping suit. For years, until they disintegrated, I managed well enough with my ex-Service striped wool pyjamas. Apart from enduring remarks about zebras wandering about in the night, they served me fine. Nowadays I have to don a track suit, put on a ski-hat, and socks, and this, plus an Adsmat, and a Black's Icelandic bag, keeps me very snug!

However, starting from scratch, I would invest in either a Helly Hanson fibre-pile suit, some 'Insulata' wear, or a set of Damart thermal underwear. This last is a complete suit, with hat and socks as well as vest and longjohns. Damart have shops in London, Manchester and Glasgow, or you can write to them at Bingley, West Yorkshire.

Of all these, the track suit is the cheapest and most adaptable, but for a really cold night in winter—for those nights when you can *hear* the frost, then a fibre-pile or Damart suit is better.

CHECK LIST

So, once again, a year-round check list:

1. Anorak or Duvet jacket with synthetic filling.
2. Cord or tweed trousers, or breeches.
3. Long wool socks.
4. Gloves and over-mitts.
5. Wool shirts and sweaters.
6. String vest and cotton underwear.
7. Boots, with cleated soles and some tri-couni nails.
8. Gaiters.
9. Walking stick or ice-axe.
10. Poncho or heavyweight cagoule.
11. Waterproof over-trousers.

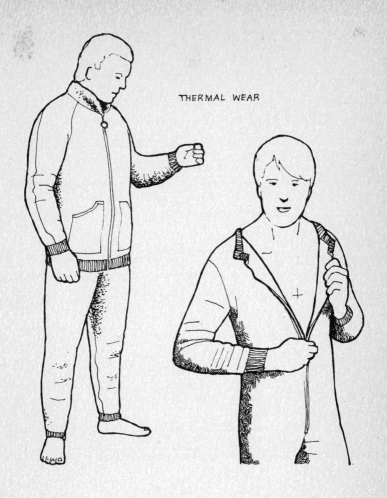

THERMAL WEAR

12. Sleeping suit, Insulata, Helly Hanson or Damart suit, and hat, plus scarf, neckerchief.

Remember that winter-weight gear is usually fine for summer use, and especially for camping at heights, as well as for normal use in winter. So with it you get the advantage of good camping gear for all sorts of weather, heights and terrains, as well as being able to use it at all times of the year.

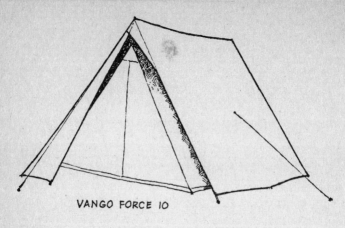

VANGO FORCE 10

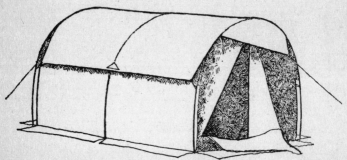

BLACK'S NYLON TUNNEL TENT

BLACKS MOUNTAIN TENT

Chapter 4

TENTS AND SLEEPING BAGS

My first tent had no flysheet, was made of cotton and had no groundsheet or porch. I had a lot of fun out of it, but if I'd known then what I know now, I'd have chosen the following:

TENT
Apart from being *well made,* the winter tent specification must include:

1. A flysheet that extends to the ground.
2. A porch.
3. A fitted groundsheet.

A FLYSHEET
With a flysheet your tent will be warmer, less prone to condensation (the bane of tent living in winter), and give much more protection against sleet and driving rain. You can, with some tents, erect and strike the inner in the shelter of the flysheet, and this is a feature worth having. *Ultimate* winter tents have this feature.

A PORCH
In the porch, you can cook, stow muddy gear, and have a sheltered spot for changing into and out of wet outer wear. A porch also protects the entrance from wind and rain.

A FITTED GROUNDSHEET
Those unaccustomed to cold weather camping can never appreciate that the greatest heat loss is from the *ground.* If, for example, you had only three blankets, you would put two under you and one on top (in fact, you would fold them into a proper sleeping bag), but get the point that it's insulation from *ground chill* that is necessary. Fitted groundsheets plus a mat, will provide this, cut down draughts, and keep rain from seeping under the tent walls. Make sure, for all these reasons, that the groundsheet is *tough.* A lightweight groundsheet is not much use, in winter. A piece of Karrimat by the door can be handy as a kneeling mat.

NYLON OR COTTON TENTS

Perhaps the best combination is a cotton inner, and a nylon fly. A cotton inner cuts down condensation, but if cotton gets damp, which is inevitable in winter, it must be *very* carefully dried and aired or it will rot. Nylon is lighter, and can be packed when wet, although you must dry and air nylon tents as well, when you get home.

Some tents have 'shower-proofed' inners, where only one side of the inner is proofed. The idea is that this is sufficient proofing to keep the rain out, while allowing the fabric to breathe. *Robert Saunders* tents, for example, have this feature.

So, when buying your tent, check that it has these 'all-weather' features. Nowadays, tent manufacture is a fast developing art, with new features and fabrics changing the situation every year. Unfortunately prices continue to increase, but in tents, as in everything else, you will only get what you pay for.

So, rather than recommend specific manufacturers or tents, we recommend that you buy from a good stockist or outdoor shop. *Pindisports, Y.H.A. Field and Trek, Brighams, Alpine Sports* or *Nevisports,* or some other shop with experienced staff will have the sort of kit you want and can advise you on specific requirements. Such shops are listed and advertised in the magazine *'Climber and Rambler'*.

Magazines like 'Camping', 'Practical Camper', and 'Climber and Rambler' regularly test tents and camping equipment, and their reports will keep you up-to-date with prices and developments, and I recommend that you buy them regularly.

SLEEPING BAGS

When I was younger there used to be advertisements for a ballpoint pen, and one of the features claimed, was that you could write with it under water. No one ever explained why anyone would *want* to write a letter underwater. The thought occurs to me because one of the current claims for sleeping bags filled with man-made fibres, is that you can sleep in it when it is soaking wet. You wring out the water, and climb in. What a grizzly thought! Would *you* like to sleep in a wet bag on a freezing night? But let's look at facts.

DOWN OR MAN-MADE FIBRES?

Down is lighter, warmer, and packs up small. If you can afford it, down has many advantages, but for year-round, or winter camping—in the U.K.—man-made fibre is better.

Sleeping bags are increasingly expensive, and if you can only

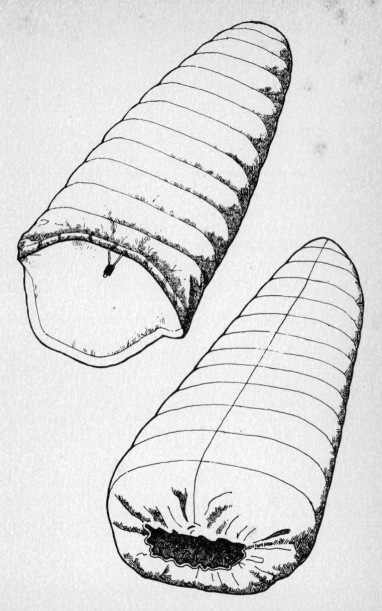

afford one, buy one with double quilting, with a synthetic filling, such as Fibrefill 2, which is the nearest artificial equivalent to down, and with the added advantage that it will retain body heat when damp or wet.

Down, you see, is fine in the dry, or even in hard frost, but when it gets wet, the feathers clog and the insulating qualities are lost. Man-made fibres are about 50% heavier than down, but even so are not too heavy.

The *Base Camp* bag, with Fibrefill 2 weights only 4 lbs 8 ozs (2.04 Kg.) while the *Thermobag* with the same filling weighs even less at 3 lbs 11 ozs (1.67 Kg), which compares very favourably with some heavyweight down bags.

A new bag, the *"Eskimo"*, from Mountain Equipment, in pile-fabric, has been widely tested and promises to be both cheaper and as effective as any available alternative. It offers controlled insulation and takes up very little space.

To sum up, it is very difficult to camp all year round in the U.K.— or anywhere else for that matter, without getting wet, or at least damp. If down gets wet, it's useless. Therefore buy a bag with man-made fibre filling, and double-quilt stitching. All bags for winter camping should have a hood, and not be *too* roomy. Use an inner. Buy from a reputable stockist, and examine the bag carefully, checking the zips and seam stitching.

AIR BEDS OR MATS
Until recently I'd always used an air bed, and Terry used a sleeping mat. For year-round use mats are better, and give more insulation.

Air beds are heavier to carry, can puncture—(especially if someone walks on it in crampons)—and when inflated are less efficient. The air inside is chilled by the ground, and then chills the underside of the bag. If you use an air bed, you must, as well as insulating the bed from the ground, insulate the sleeping bag from the bed.

Mats like the *Adsmat* or *Karrimat* are good, because they are thick enough to stop the ground chill striking through to the bag. Even if you don't use a bed or mat in the summer, one or the other is essential in the winter.

BITS AND PIECES:
TENT PEGS
The ground can freeze rock-hard in the winter. You need stout, steel pegs and something to hammer them in with. On the other hand it can get very wet and muddy, and pegs won't hold. For this

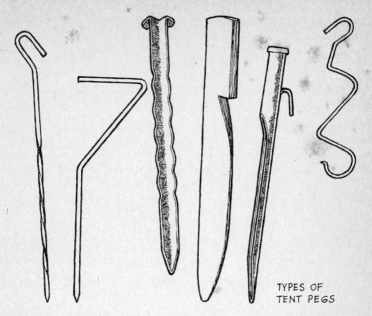

TYPES OF
TENT PEGS

you need extra long pegs, in aluminium or plastic, with serrated edges.

So take a *selection* of pegs—at least enough for the main guys.

EXTRA GUYS
Strong winds and driving rain play havoc with guy ropes. Take extra line to really lash the tent down.

PLASTIC SHEETS
Plastic bags are cheap, light, and for the winter camper, indispensable. Get big ones. When not in use spread them on the tent floor—it all helps insulation. Have one for draping over your bag if the rain beats in during the night.

I woke up once, on the Cairngorms, to find that so much rain had beaten in that I was afloat, on my air bed, on top of a mountain! The snow had melted under the tent, and in the hollow this had formed, Terry and I bobbed about. The rain had beaten in on my side, so I floated wet, while he floated dry—curse him!

When I moaned about this to Alan Blackshaw, who was in the tent next door, he said airily that *he* always had a plastic sheet draped on the windward wall of the tent, so that whatever else happened, the rain couldn't drive in. There's a tip from an expert, and one I have never forgotten. (Tips you learn the hard way you tend to remember).

J-CLOTHS
Condensation is the menace in winter camping. Keep the inner walls away from the fly, ventilate well, cook in the porch, and when all else fails, keep mopping the walls with a J-cloth, obtainable from most grocery stores and ironmongers.

CHECK LIST
1. Winter tent in nylon with:—
   a) flysheet
   b) porch
   c) fitted groundsheet

2. Sleeping bag with:—
   a) double quilt stitching
   b) mad-made fibre filling
   c) a hood

   Black's, Mountain Equipment, Pointfive, and *Polywarm* are all sound makes.

3. A sleeping pad—full length.
4. Extra pegs:
   a) steel for hard ground
   b) plastic, wood or aluminium for mud.
5. Extra rope for guying.
6. Plastic bags, sheets and J-cloths for fighting condensation.

COST
Its not cheap. However, if you buy at end of summer sales, or from shops giving special offers, you should be able to acquire the basics for £150—and there is always Father Christmas!

Chapter 5

KIT FOR COOKING AND LIGHTING

STOVES

If I was equipping myself for winter camping, I wouldn't buy a gas stove. The gas is butane, which will not gasify at –0°C, and burns less than enthusiastically if it just gets cold. Moreover, you have to cart full cylinders out, and empty ones back.

Having said that, it's fair to add that for most camping I prefer gas. It's cleaner and saves carting fuel in cans or bottles. But it's not the best for the winter. For the same reason we don't favour solid fuel. It is fine for picnics and mid-morning brews, but gives off fumes, and is too slow in the winter.

WINTER SPECIFICATION

A winter stove should run off petrol, paraffin or meths. *Trangia* meths stoves are highly thought of, and come in sets which contain a burner, a support and windshield, and a cooking pot.

Paraffin or petrol stoves, from *SVEA* or *Primus/Optimus* have been around for years, and are very suitable for the winter camper. They come in various sizes of half, and one pint capacity. The aim must be to avoid duplicating your fuel and for this reason we prefer an *Optimus* paraffin stove because for lighting we prefer a paraffin fuelled lantern. Thus one fuel gives us heat, cooking and light.

Your specification for winter then, demands a stove which will:—
1. Burn at low temperatures.
2. Have a windshield.
3. Share a common fuel.
4. Run on petrol, paraffin or meths.

Remember that to carry petrol, you must have it in a metal container. Unless the container is marked PETROL, garages *may,* and certainly should, refuse to fill it for you. Have a small plastic funnel for filling the stove for you don't want petrol spilling. *NEVER* fill or light a stove inside your tent.

Incidentally, use the *lowest* grade fuel you can get. Four-star petrol is too heavily leaded for stoves; two-star fuel will burn better and cause less trouble with jets. The popular Optimus 8R will burn leaded or unleaded fuel, is self-pricking, and self-regulating.

Most petrol and paraffin pressure stoves have to be primed. Meta fuel tablets or Optimus burning paste is better than meths for this purpose.

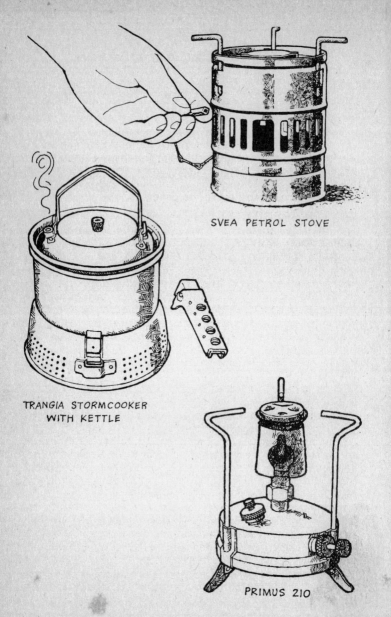

SVEA PETROL STOVE

TRANGIA STORMCOOKER
WITH KETTLE

PRIMUS 210

32

SPARES

If your stove is not self-pricking, you need to carry one or two prickers, and a few washers for valves and fuel cocks are useful. Pressure stoves *must* be well maintained, for safety's sake.

LIGHTING

In the winter, depending on where you are, it is dark by about 4.00 p.m. (1600 hrs.) and stays dark until 7.00 a.m. (0700 hrs.) the next day. That's 15 hours, and it takes some thinking about!

This fact alone indicates that you will need some form of lighting, not just for convenience, but for safety.

TORCHES

As a hand-torch, you need one with a wide, rather than a spot beam, and with some way of attaching it to belt or tent, so that you can use it with both hands free. The angle-head Scout-torch is popular, light, (11 ozs) and runs for hours.

For tent lighting—if you like reading or have notes to write up, something larger might be better instead (not as well). *Ever-Ready* have a wide range of torches, and you can see a selection in any electrical shop.

BULBS AND BATTERIES

Carry spare bulbs (2) and one extra set of batteries. Reverse the batteries in the case, so that they won't be drained if the torch gets switched on accidentally. Remove the batteries from the torch when you get home, as even leak-proof batteries seem to ooze. If the torch gets wet, dry it carefully or rust will ruin it.

CANDLES

Providing you are careful, there is a lot to be said for candles. They are light, last a long time, and even give a little heat. In a snow hole they are ideal.

Buy short, squat, long-life, camping candles—like a super nightlight, rather than the thin, unsteady household variety. Put the candle in a pot or pan, taller than the candle, and seal it down with wax. Then if it falls over, it's inside the pot and safe.

LANTERNS

Family campers swear by the *Tilley Storm lantern*. It is excellent, but it's heavy (4 lbs) (1 kilo 75 g). Hurricane lamps, running on paraffin are smaller, lighter, have a wick rather than a mantle, and you can share the fuel with an Optimus 96 or III type stove, which runs on paraffin.

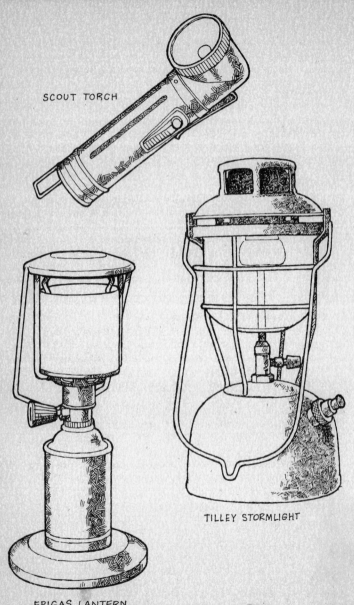

SCOUT TORCH

EPIGAS LANTERN

TILLEY STORMLIGHT

34

You can also buy gas lanterns like the *Lumogaz 'C'* or *Epi-gas* models. Remember, if you are cooking and lighting by gas cylinder, you *MUST NOT,* in most cases, unscrew the pierced cylinder from the stove burner to screw it on the lighting head. *Never* unscrew a partly full, pierced gas container. *Epi-gas* has a converter unit, with which you can swap a stove head for a lantern. Always check the manufacturer's instructions. Gas containers are fine, provided you can keep them *warm,* and really you need something to keep *you* warm.

HEATING

The first heat *source* is food, which we will discuss later. The next point, heat *retention,* is answered by having the right gear, and using it correctly. The third, *external* heat, we will look at now.

A candle, or a paraffin lantern will give off quite useful amounts of heat, and if you are in your bag, properly clad, munching a chocolate bar or drinking coffee laced with rum, while reading this book, however frosty it is outside, you'll be in paradise!

My good friend, Robin Adshead, backpacker supreme, swears by his *ALP* gaslantern, both for light and heat. Hot enough to dry your socks by, and weighs only 12 ozs (340 grams).

The snag with heating the inside of the tent is that it leads to condensation, but this is often an acceptable snag.

COOKSETS

In winter, it is quite essential that all your pots and pans have lids. Food will go icy on top, water will be slow to boil, and fat can sputter about, if you don't have and use a lid, and you can eat off it, or use a plate as a lid (unless it's plastic), but keep food covered while it's cooking, or it will be a slow, cold meal.

LIGHTING AND COOKING CHECK LIST
STOVES:
1. Petrol, paraffin or meths.   2. With windshield.
3. Share a fuel source with light or heat.

LIGHTING:
1. Hand-torch or tent-torch capable of attaching to tent or clothing.
2. Long-life candles (use in pot).
3. Paraffin hurricane lamp, with wick.
4. Spare bulbs and batteries.

HEATING:
1. Lantern or candles.   2. ALP gas lantern.

Chapter 6

FIRST STEPS IN WINTER CAMPING

We have now devoted half this book to equipment. We have covered what you need to amplify your summer gear, with the extra kit you don't need in summer, but which is essential in winter. We have also covered the specifications for gear you would buy if you were starting camping from scratch with every intention of camping in heat-wave and blizzard.

This may have given you the impression that the winter camper humps tons of extra gear, and is loaded like a mule. This is not the case, although it is fair to say that because your gear needs to be more robust, and you do need some extra items, you will carry more, which will, of course, weigh more.

When we were lads, the accent was all on technique. There wasn't much choice in gear, and you coped with weather by picking careful sites and using fieldcraft. We're not certain that the current emphasis on equipment is either desirable or necessary, especially if it leads to the neglect of outdoor skills. So let's look at techniques.

FIRST STEPS IN WINTER CAMPING

The place to start is a frosty night in November-December in your back garden.

Pitch the tent in the late afternoon and go out about 7 or 8 p.m. with your stove, get inside and carefully brew yourself a cup of tea. When you crawl out again, and shine your torch on the roof, you will most probably see that the roof is smudged with damp patches in the sparkling frost, where the flysheet has touched the inner walls. At each patch, condensation will be forming on the inside. You will also discover that it is hard work forcing pegs into frozen ground, that poles are chilly to handle, and that as you lie on the groundsheet brewing up, the cold is striking up at you from the ground. You must adjust the fly to get the cold fly off the warm(ish) inner. Points of contact lead to condensation.

Your first steps in winter camping should be taken either as suggested, in the back garden, or on some pitch close to home. In this way you can discover the snags, fairly painlessly, before you strike out for a full trip away, somewhere remote.

FINDING A PITCH

In winter, the site needs to have rather different features from a summer site, and the first difference is that you must have a site organized at least *one hour before dusk, which means by about 3.00 p.m.!*

In summer it's nice to pitch in a breezy spot, to keep the tent cool and aired. In winter the first requirement is for a sheltered pitch. Avoid hollows, for they attract and retain frost, can be boggy, and if it rains on hard ground, could fill with water. Under trees is also inadvisable, for in the morning, when the temperature rises, you will have to endure a rain of heavy drops, from bare frosty branches, and the ground is usually soggy and a mash of wet leaves. Under a cliff you may have stones falling on you in a thaw. In the lee of a wall, facing east, on well drained soil, would be ideal. One theory is that the morning sun will dry the condensation before you pack the tent up. In winter this does not always happen. In fact, a typical morning usually looks like this:—

When you crawl out, the outer fly is white with frost, and if you peer between inner and fly, you will see heavy condensation frozen on the inner fly wall. Worse, when you crawl out of the tent, cold air rushes in, and condensation freezes on the *inside inner* wall. So you end up with a fairly well-iced tent. But more of this anon.

AVOID PITCHING
UNDER TREES
IN HOLLOWS
AT THE FOOT OF CLIFFS.

PITCHING

In winter it is very important to pitch the tent fast or you will probably have to pitch in the dark. Practise this in the garden.

A good routine for a wet, windy day, goes as follows:—

1. Select a site with shelter from the wind. Put the rucksack in some sheltered spot, to unpack the tent.

2. If possible, pitch the fly, and then the inner.

3. Pitch at *right-angles* to the wind. It is better to have the wind blowing on the side of the tent rather than getting under the fly and into the tent and wrenching all away. Opinions vary on this point, but this is ours. You will discover by experiment which way suits the circumstances of the moment.

4. To peg out the tent in the wind, *lie on it.* Simply slap the tent down, and lie on it. It's the only way to keep the tent from blowing away, while having your hands free to get the pegs in.

If the ground is soggy, you will need to use deep wooden pegs, or long plastic ones. Thin steel pegs won't hold in wet ground. Steel pegs may need to be hammered in with a rock, in really icy conditions, and if they won't go in, you will need to find *very* heavy stones to guy on to.

INSULATION

You can't have too much insulation. You can cut bracken or reeds to put under the tent, if any are available. We usually spread the 10' x 6' plastic survival sheet on the ground, *under* the groundsheet. In cold weather it keeps the damp down and keeps mud off the groundsheet bottom, mud that otherwise ends up smeared over the inner when you pack up. This is an example of the great winter camping rule:—

Whenever possible, every item should serve two purposes.

Inside, newspapers spread on the deck will provide great

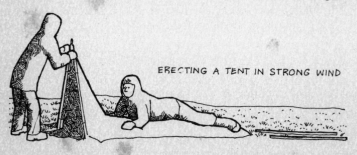

ERECTING A TENT IN STRONG WIND

insulation and keep the mud at bay; you can also read them by lamplight — another dual purpose achieved! A piece of foam or Karrimat is excellent insulation.

Spread out mats or inflate airbeds, then unpack the rucksacks. Stow gear round the walls, while you sleep in the middle.

Sleeping bags should be unrolled, and shaken. This will give the filling time to loft, and improve the insulating qualities.

STOWING GEAR

Some folks leave as much gear as possible in the rucksack, and keep it in the tent porch, covered with the cagoule, or a plastic bag. The snag is that if you need anything later, you have to come out into the cold and rain to get it. We recommend unpacking the rucksack completely, strapping it up again and putting it under the fly.

Cooking gear, fuel (except gas), tinned food and any bulky or muddy items can be left in the porch, but covered up with plastic bags or sheets. Cagoules can be left there if wet, but should be wiped dry and brought in if possible, to serve either as more insulation, as a barrier against condensation drips, or in case you have to go out again.

Don't leave boots outside, in cold weather. They will set like rocks overnight, be difficult to put on, and *very* chilly. Clean them off and wrap them in plastic. They are awkward, but you can't do without them!

WET GEAR

If you get wet during the day, stay wet. Change into dry clothes when you stop for the night, and not before. Wring out any wet gear, socks etc., and hang them up somewhere, on loops sewn into the roof if possible. You *can* buy heaters like the ALP lantern, which give out enough heat to dry gear, but it's extra weight. Sensible use of waterproofs during the day and a change into dry clothes at night is the best answer. You may have to put damp clothes on again in the morning (ugh!) but you will soon warm up.

PLASTIC BAGS/NEWSPAPERS

If we were asked to name two useful items for the winter camper, then newspapers and plastic bags would get strong consideration. They may not be very environmental, but they are incredibly useful and very light.

So, here we are, a sheltered pitch, tent up, insulation down, bag unrolled, into warm gear. Not so bad, is it?

What's next?

Chapter 7

FOOD

COOKING

In winter you need hot food. Salads, cheese and apples won't do. Don't cook in the tent. It's not a good idea at any time, but in winter the few obvious advantages are far outweighed by the many less obvious disadvantages, chief of which are fire risk, mess, heavy condensation, and danger from fumes and carbon monoxide. Cook outside, or in foul weather, in the lee of the porch.

MATCHES/LIGHTERS

It's best to have both. Matches are affected by damp, and if you put them inside a shirt pocket, perspiration and body warmth will ruin them just as effectively as rainwater.

Buy a box of red-top matches, and split the contents and striker. Put them into any small sealed container. We use film cassette boxes. Colour film comes in either metal screw-top boxes, or plastic ones with snap-on lids. You can (if very keen) glue the striker inside the lid with double-sided sticking tape, but otherwise you remove striker and match and strike them together. Always re-close the boxes, remembering to replace the striker. Note that you need two lots seperately sealed and stored.

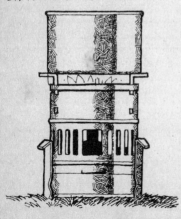

STOVE CHOCKED AGAINST THE
WIND WITH TENT PEGS
DRIVEN IN EITHER SIDE.

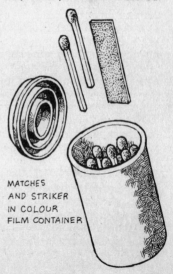

MATCHES
AND STRIKER
IN COLOUR
FILM CONTAINER

LIGHTER

Petrol lighters are best. Get one with a big windshield, the American Zippo being excellent.

Once you have a stove, and the means to light it, it is very important to stand the stove on firm ground, chocking it with stones if possible.

Shelter the stove from wind. In winter the wind is *cold*. It will disperse the heat from the burner, so a windshield on the stove is essential. An asbestos blanket can be a very useful windshield, draped over stove and cook-pot. Remember also that a gust of wind can blow the pot off the stove, so be sure you have both cooker and pot secure.

You will cook your food faster if you have lids for all pots. A metal plate can serve as a lid, and this gets the plate warm as well — another double use!

FOOD

With the proviso that you want to go for high calorie foods, like those listed below, your normal foods will probably be sufficient, but you will need more food in winter. Food is your prime heat source, so don't stint on it.

Muesli or porridge makes a good start to the day with a couple of boiled eggs, and a good mug of tea or coffee. Never start a day's hike in winter without a good breakfast inside you. To do so is an invitation to exposure.

Having got off to a good start, eat or nibble regularly throughout the day. Chocolate, Mars bars, a handful of raisins or nuts, or boiled sweets, all high in calories, will keep the internal furnace burning away all day.

If it's raining or cold, you won't want to make long stops. It's better to cut out a mid-morning brew, but eat steadily through the day and have a good meal at night — which is only 5 p.m. If you find a sheltered spot for a mid-day meal, fine, but otherwise press on.

Fried food is best avoided, although if your idea of camping is the smell of frying bacon, then fry away. Don't fry food inside the tent though. If fat sputters on tent walls or sleeping bags, it will do severe damage to the fabric. The same thing applies when cooking in the porch.

A good stew, lots of meat or spaghetti, mashed potatoes, and some rice pudding, will give you a real glow to start the night on.

Dehydrated food is light, and of increasing variety. Just add water and heat, following the instructions on the packet, and you have a nourishing meal.

Before turning in, or once in bed, have half a mug of tea or coffee, and some chocolate, or a few wholewheat biscuits—not very good for the teeth, but it will see you warmly through the night.

The snag with drinking lots of tea is that you usually then have to turn out in the night for a pee. It's often better to remember this and cut down on the fluids once you have settled down for the night.

FOOD LIST

We're not going to give you recipes or even cooking hints. There is a wide range of foods and you can learn how to cook them by reading the instructions on the labels. It is essential to eat food of high calorific value, and apart from the usual items — milk, sugar, etc., your diet is best chosen from the following list:

HIGH CALORIE FOOD SELECTION

Breakfast:
Muesli with milk/porridge with milk and brown sugar.
Tinned fish, like sardines.
Eggs.
Cheese.
Tea/Coffee with milk.

During the Day:
(Fuel Food)
Chocolate.
Mars bars.
Raisins/Currants
Nuts.
Boiled Glucose sweets.

Main Meal:
Thick soups.
Meat stews.
Spaghetti or Pasta.
Rice puddings, milk and brown sugar.
Mashed potatoes.
Dried Fruit.

Supper:
Cheese with wholewheat biscuits.
Chocolate.
Hot drinks.

Plus: Tea/coffee. And don't forget your knife, fork and spoon and a *tin-opener*.

You can buy some of this food in dehydrated form. Try and avoid too many tins. one tin a day, say of stew or thick soup, is quite enough weight, and will give you a good boost.

You can buy convenience foods in most outdoor shops. This includes milk in tubes or dried milk in packets. Tea- or coffee-bags are better than loose tea or coffee, and brown sugar is better than white.

WEIGHT
You can get by, quite comfortably on about 2 lbs (1 kilo) of food a day. So for two people, over a weekend, you should aim to keep your food weight for Friday night to Sunday afternoon to about 5 lbs of food each.

WATER
Contrary to popular belief it is *more* difficult to find water — that is, fresh, pure water — in the winter. There is plenty of mud, but if it is cold, ponds and lakes can be frozen — certainly close to the bank. Horse troughts can be covered with thick ice, and many pumps and taps are turned off in case they freeze and burst. So you must aim to take water with you, and as you will spend more time in the tent, drinking a brew, you'll need more water. Snow is a useful substitute, but if you try melting it, it will melt quicker if you add a little water. Whenever possible, melt ice rather than snow.

Chapter 8

PROBLEMS

It is no good pretending that winter camping is the pleasant, balmy, sun-kissed, idyllic pastime that summer camping is *supposed* to be. We'd say that winter camping is *different* from summer camping, and has pleasures of its own. But there are problems. Let's make a few suggestions to deal specifically with them.

CONDENSATION

Yes, folks, it's back with condensation again! If you have only camped in summer, you cannot believe just how much condensation you can get in a tent in winter. You may have to mop it up and *wring out* the cloth. There is no cure, but there are a few rules which will help.

1. The fly must not touch the inner.
2. Ventilate the tent as much as possible.
3. Mop the drips with J-cloths continually.

Newspapers are handy. They soak up the moisture on the groundsheet, and newspapers spread over the sleeping bag will absorb moisture, and let the bag breathe. Those tramps on the Thames Embankment know about winter, poor devils, and they use newspapers for warmth as well as necessity.

RAIN

Pick a good sheltered site. Don't camp in stream-beds or gulleys. They may be sheltered, but they are dangerous in winter.

Have a tent where the fly can go up first and come down last and you can work in the shelter. If it rains heavily you may have to trench around the tent. A careful choice of site is the best answer, especially from driving rain. You must get some sort of lee out of the wind. If you get flooded out, leap from the sleeping bag and stow that first. You don't want to drown in it and you don't want it wet. Put on the waterproofs before going out and secure anything — like plates, maps, or air beds, likely to float away.

WIND

It's surprising how much shelter from the wind exists, if you look around properly. When you are standing up, being buffeted about, all six feet of you, you tend to forget that your tent is usually less than waist high.

So kneel down. You will find shelter at this level, in what at first just appears to be the most exposed situation. Low walls, copses, hedges, haystacks or buildings, even folds in the ground, can all make good lees.

DOUBLE GUYING

It's a sensible precaution to put extra guys on in winter, especially if winds are forecast. You run the guys out from the poles to well spread pegs. Brace the pegs in to resist the heaving that the wind will give to the guying.

We find that two guys run out to windward help to brace the tent against buffeting. If any are available, pile rocks around the pegs, and the skirt of the tent.

HARD, ROCKY OR FROZEN GROUND, SNOW

Steel pegs will penetrate all but rock, but can be worked loose by the wind. Even on flinty ground you can work a peg in somewhere, but if it is rock you have a problem. Try lifting a few rocks, then there may be enough earth underneath to take a peg, and it may not be frozen so hard. Ice-axes can support the end guys, in soft ground or deep snow.

If you can't get a peg in and have to attach the guys to rocks, make sure the rocks are big. Those you can barely get your arms around are better than those the size of house bricks. The rule for rocks is the bigger, the better, but don't strain yourself!

MUD

Mud gets everywhere. Keep it out of the tent. Fortunately mud does no permanent harm, but it's far from pleasant, and most winter campers prefer hard frozen days to murky rainy ones, when they squelch about in slop. Go for well drained pitches and avoid making tracks around the tent. Your feet will churn up the pitch so the less movement about the site, the better. Go for short grass slopes, with good drainage, as your camp site.

If the site is very muddy, spread your survival sheet *under* the ground sheet. Then, in the morning you can, with luck, fold up the tent with a clean bottom, and only have a muddy plastic sheet to sluice down and stow in a bag.

ICE AND VERGLAS

Ice is not too much of a problem, but be careful of trusting your weight to it when filling water bottles or washing plates. Remember that with 40 lbs on your back you will go through ice that would support you unloaded. Verglas on hill tracks is a menace, and can always be anticipated if fog comes down over about 1000 feet. Use a walking stick and pick your footholds carefully. Nailed boots are preferable in the hills in winter.

SNOW

If you can, keep off snow slopes, Never trek in the hills in winter without an ice-axe and crampons. Know how to use the ice-axe for braking if you slip on a snow slope.

Apart from the dangers of a slip while walking, and perhaps an avalanche if you are camped in a snow-filled corrie — where you shouldn't be in the first place — snow is to be welcomed by winter campers.

It's clean, warmer than a hard frost, and makes for easy windbreaks. Pegs are a problem in snow, as they work loose. Bury them deep, and put stones on top. Dust the snow off before you enter the tent, or it will melt everywhere. You want to wear gaiters in snow to keep boots, socks and trouser bottoms dry.

MIST AND FOG

Mist and fog, with overcast skies have one great disadvantage. It gets dark earlier. They also make navigation difficult, and can damp gear down into claminess.

The lower slopes of hills will keep you out of low cloud, which clings round the tops.

Navigation, especially in remote areas is not helped by poor visibility. Your map and compass work must be of a high standard, and if it isn't can we recommend *The Spur Book of Map and Compass'*, and lots of practice.

GUY RUN TO
ICE AXE DEEP
IN SNOW

PEG FROZEN IN
BY POURING
WATER OVER

Chapter 9

SAFETY FIRST
FIRST AID: MAP AND COMPASS WEATHER LORE

These three subjects are also the titles of three of our Venture
Guides, which we recommend to you. *'Survival and Rescue'*,
another title, would also be useful. The subjects they deal with all
have particular relevance in the winter, so let's just look briefly
here at the winter camping aspects.

FIRST AID KIT
The First Aid kit should contain:—

1. Squares of lint or gauze.
2. Roller bandages in various widths.
3. A tin of plasters, plus 'Moleskin' for blisters.
4. Several larger plasters.
5. A roll of sticking plaster.
6. A fistful of cottonwool.
7. Three or four safety pins.
8. A tube of Savlon.
9. Some bicarbonate of soda.
10. A small pair of scissors.
11. Vaseline and Nivea cream or something similar, and a lip
    salve.

These last items are a useful preventative in winter. Cold winds
will sear your face, chap the backs of your hands and crack
your lips.

None of this is deadly, but any fool can be uncomfortable! A
smear of Vaseline on the face and a rub of salve on the lips can
help the day and night pass much more comfortably.

One thing that *is* deadly, and a permanent danger in the winter
is hypothermia (exposure). So note the following:—

HYPOTHERMIA
This is caused by a combination of:—

1. Inadequate diet (no breakfast etc.).
2. Wind chill.
3. Wet clothing.

47

4. Inadequate clothing.

5. Physical tiredness.

The symptoms are:—

Lagging behind, stumbling or falling down; slurred speech or moroseness; uncharacteristic behaviour — ("What's up with Jim today?"); stupidity or dullness; sudden bursts of uncharacteristic chatter.

All these are symptoms and if you notice them in yourself or others during the weather conditions described, then you, or your companions must act at once.

1. Stop.

2. Get the casualty out of the wind, for example by putting up the tent. Then if the casualty is still conscious —

3. Get him warm. Strip off wet clothing, and put on dry. Get him into a sleeping bag and if you can, cram someone else in as well. Cover the head and hands (30% of all heat loss is from the head). Make a hot drink and *if he is conscious* get it into him.

If the hypothermia victim has become unconscious, he is in serious trouble, and you must get a doctor at once.

WIND CHILL

Low temperatures in themselves are no real problem if you are adequately clad, and keep moving. However, if the wind gets up, as can easily happen in cold, frosty weather, then the *effective* temperature is much lower than the true air temperature. At say, -1°C a 20 mile an hour wind gives an *effective temperature much below the true air temperature of -1°C*, and that can be lethal if you are not prepared for it. Watch out for wind chill.

WIND CHILL CHART

Wind Speed	Local Temperature (F)			
0	32	23	14	5
5	29	20	10	1
10	18	7	-4	-15
15	13	-1	-13	-25
20	7	-6	-19	-32
30	1	-13	-27	-41

FROSTBITE

There is not a great risk of frostbite, but the extremities, feet, hands and ears get very chilled. Chilblains are a problem. The basic cause of chilblains is poor circulation, and too tight garments. Be sure your toes can wriggle. Keep the ears and nose covered if a chill wind is blowing, and wear gloves.

If you do lose sensation from ears or fingers, don't rub snow on the deadened part, or indeed rub the area at all. You can flay the skin off. Cup your warm hands over the spot, put fingers under your armpits, and warm the area gently.

The important thing for all campers in winter and summer, is that they should know First Aid, and apply it at once in emergencies.

MAP AND COMPASS

Except on cold frosty days, visibility is usually poor in winter, and this causes map reading problems. Leafless woods lose their identifiable shape, snow flattens everything out, mist closes in and makes features difficult to identify.

The sum total of this is that you have to rely more on compass bearings and contours, since those churches with tower or steeple which you rely on in summertime, are often invisible in winter.

The winter camper must take frequent bearings, and *always* know his position. Mist and fog can close in with great rapidity and once it does you can soon be lost, with unpleasant consequences.

You must be competent with map and compass and, as usual, the first rule is to 'set' or 'orient' the map and keep it 'set'.

Some other skills which must be thoroughly learned are as follows:—

RESECTION

Before you go camping, both in winter and in summer, you should know how to find and give a map reference and how to calculate a bearing, and understand a little about contours. The compass is the most important item in poor visibility, but it helps to know a little about the terrain.

Open the map out and look at it from a distance of two or three paces. Try and get an overall impression of the land it represents, which way the streams flow, where the woods are, and so on.

To find your position you need two or more identifiable features of landmarks on the ground, that you can also find on the map.

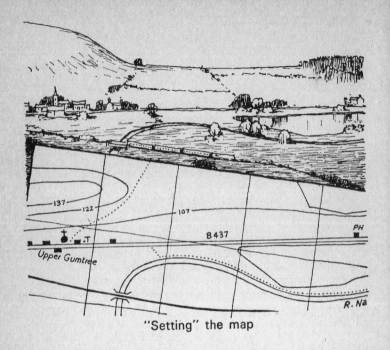

"Setting" the map

These should preferably be some distance apart, at right-angles to each other, so that you have cross-bearings to fix your position. This is called 'resection'.

You may know where your landmarks are on the map and ground, but you don't know where you are. To find out, take the following action.

Take the compass in the left hand and point the Travel arrow directly at the landmark. Then, holding the compass steady, swivel the compass housing until the needle and orienting arrow match, North to North. The bearing of the landmark can now be read off the dial at the Index pointer mark. Note this bearing down.

Repeat this with the second and subsequent landmarks, until you have two or more magnetic bearings, from your position to two identifiable landmarks.

Note this carefully. These are *magnetic* or compass bearings. They need to be converted into *grid bearings* by removing the magnetic variation.

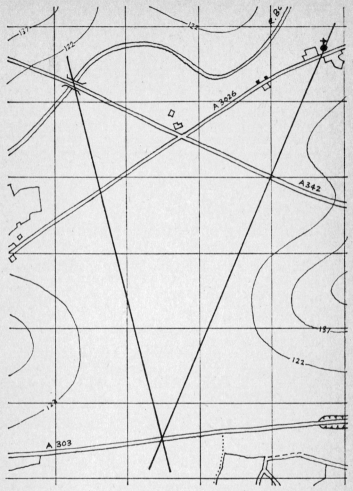

Your position by resection

NOTE: To convert *grid* bearings to *magnetic* bearings you ADD the variation (GUMA). To convert a *magnetic* bearing to a *grid* bearing you subtract (MUGS).

GUMA — Grid Unto Magnetic = Add

or:

MUGS — Magnetic Unto Grid = Subtract

The mnemonic GUMA or MUGS, from the first letter of each word is one way of remembering what to do to convert bearings. People frequently make mistakes in converting bearings, and this may help you to get it right.

In the present case we have to *subtract* the magnetic variation from the magnetic bearing, to get a grid bearing. So, if our magnetic bearings were 300° and 50° respectively and the magnetic variation was 8°, our grid bearings would be 292° and 42° respectively.

These are the bearings from your position to the landmarks, from a point you cannot identify to two (or more) points you can. You can find your position as follows:—

Set the first magnetic bearing on the dial of the compass, and then deduct the variation. This automatically gives you the grid bearing. Forget the compass bearing, you no longer need it. Place the compass on the map. Place the direction line over the first landmark, with the landmark as close to the compass dial as possible. Then, keeping the sighting line over the landmark, swivel the compass until the *orienting lines* are parallel with the *grid lines* with the orienting arrow pointing North. Next, at the point where the sighting line runs off the compass, mark the map with a dot, making a map mark.

Now, using the edge of the compass as a ruler, draw a pencil line connecting the map mark and the landmark, and run it back towards you. Your position is somewhere along that line.

Repeat the process on the second landmark. The line from this point should cut the first line, and where they cut, you are.

Remember the steps:—

1. Identify two or more landmarks on the ground and on the map.
2. Take magnetic bearings.
3. Deduct the magnetic variation to make a grid bearing.
4. Set these bearings on the compass and draw in a series of intersecting lines on the map.
5. Where the lines intersect is your position.

Now, so far, we have used the compass to set the map, and to find your position. The same process can be used to march between two points. This may seem irrelevant, for, when you can see your landmark or object, why do you need a compass bearing to reach it? However, if you wanted to reach it through a thick wood, in fog, or at night, then a compass bearing to march on would be invaluable.

GRID BEARINGS INTO MAGNETIC OR COMPASS BEARINGS

To obtain a grid bearing, you have first to identify your position, and your objective on the map.

Lay the edge of the compass down as a line to connect these two points, then turn the compass housing until the orienting lines are parallel to the grid lines. Ignore the compass needle at this point.

You can now read off the grid bearing at the index pointer. Remember this is a grid bearing, and to convert it into a magnetic or compass bearing, you have to ADD the magnetic variation i.e., grid unto magnetic add, or GUMA.

Let us say that the magnetic variation is again 8°, so if your grid bearing is 250, you add 8°, and set the compass dial to 258.

You can now put the map away, and, taking the compass in the left hand, simply swivel yourself around until the North point of the magnetic needle, centres over the North point of the orienting arrow. To march in the correct direction, you keep the needles together and start off, in the direction indicated by the travel arrow.

MARCHING ON A COMPASS BEARING

This is the real crux of map and compass work; the process of calculating a bearing on a map, translating it on to the compass, and then, using both compass and map, marching to and arriving at your destination, easily, economically and safely, in all weathers, day or night, and especially in winter. Most of the steps will be already familiar to you, but are well worth going over once again. The steps to take are these:—

1. Find your position, by compass or visual checks, and set the map.

2. Find your destination on the map and plot a course to it. If the destination lies across a river, or over a cliff, you may need to go by various 'legs' or 'stages', to reach a bridge or ford. The process for each leg is the same.

3. Link up the points by a pencil line, or if the distance is not too far, the edge of the Silva compass.

4. Lay the edge of the Silva compass along this pencil line and then turn the compass housing until the orienting lines are parallel with the grid lines. Ignore the compass needle at this point.

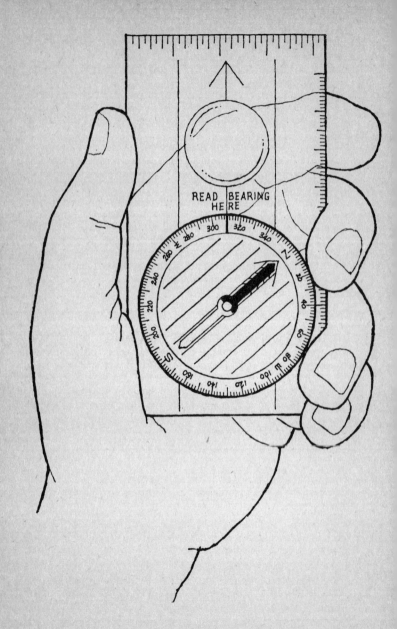

54

5. The grid bearing can be read off the compass dial, at the sighting line point.

6. ADD the magnetic variation (GUMA).

7. Taking the compass in the left hand, turn until the compass needle coincides with the orienting needle, North to North.

8. Keeping these two aligned, walk off in the direction indicated by the travel arrow.

BACKBEARINGS

Backbearings can be very useful in map marching, or in checking your position. A backbearing, as the name implies, is the bearing in the opposite direction to your objective, and you calculate it very simply as follows:

There are 360° on a compass dial, 180° West, 180° East. To get the backbearings of a particular bearing, you simply, if it is less than 180°, add 180°, and if it is more than 180°, subtract 180°. For example:—

Bearing 270° Backbearing (less 180°)   =   90°

Bearing 60° Backbearing (plus 180°)   =   240°

What is the use of it? Imagine you are on a steep hill, overlooking a flat plain, and you have to cross it on a bearing of 150°. When you are out in the middle of the plain you may have no object ahead of you to line up on, and can start to wander off line. However, if you keep the hill you started from behind you on a constant bearing of 330°, you know you are still on the right line for your objective.

You can use this technique to fix your position, by using the backbearing from an object to fix your position, or, if the backbearing cuts another point behind you, to establish your line.

Also, if you are marching on an objective, mist may obscure the objective ahead, while the point you have left is still clear. Again, if you realise suddenly that you are lost, you can retrace your route along the backbearing until you recognise where you are.

CONTOURS

A map is a pictorial representation of the ground, but while the map is flat, the ground is bumpy; not to mention rolling, hilly or mountainous. These changes in the level, or relief of the land are indicated on O.S. maps by contour lines.

Contours are quite easy to follow, provided you grasp the idea that a contour is an imaginary line following the surface of the ground at a specific level. The contour follows the same height

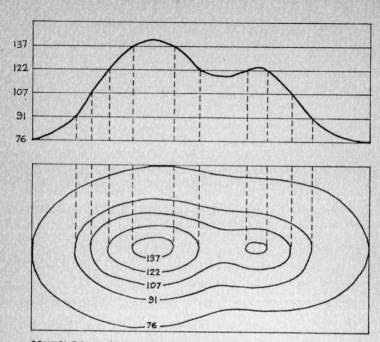

CONTOURS OF A HILL WITH A COL

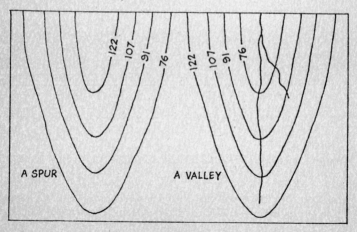

A SPUR

A VALLEY

DIFFERENCE BETWEEN A SPUR AND A VALLEY OR RE-ENTRANT

Contour lines

round the hills, into the re-entrants, but they can give you a very good idea of the shape of the land. On the 1:50,000 O.S. map the contour lines are 50 feet apart. Therefore, if the lines are close together it follows that the land is rising very quickly. If far apart, that the slope is gentle. If at irregular intervals that the land undulates.

One point that foxes people is to know from the contour lines whether the land is rising or falling, whether a feature is a spur or re-entrant. A spur projects from the land mass, while a re-entrant is exactly the opposite i.e., a shallow valley reaching into the mass. Apart from experience these points will help. Firstly, the contour values, which are given to the nearest metre, are given so that they read facing uphill. Remember though, that while the heights are in metres, the contour lines are 50 feet apart. Secondly, you can compare contour values which are given at regular intervals along the line. Thirdly, commonsense. Rivers and streams do not normally run up spurs or along the tops of hills. Often other features will give you the clue.

Apart from contours, height is indicated by *spot heights* which are indicated on the map as follows: °117. This is the precise height, in metres, above sea level at this particular point. You will also find *trig points*, indicated on the map as follows: △180. This again is the exact height above sea level, and on the spot you will find a concrete triangular obelisk with metal fittings in the top. This supported surveying instruments when the map was made.

Finally, apart from contour lines, very steep slopes or cliffs are shown by a visual reproduction of a cliff, or a series of sharp jagged arrowheads. Be wary of areas like this when out on the ground in poor weather.

TIME AND DISTANCE

Your wristwatch — with luminous dial, is a useful aid in winter. With a compass bearing and Naismith's rule you can calculate your position fairly accurately in the worst weather.

Naismith's Rule: Every winter camper ought to know and apply Naismith's Rule for cross-country walking. The basic rule gives an unloaded speed of 3 mph plus half an hour for each thousand feet climbed. With 40 lbs on your back you won't do that on the flat. On a winter's day 12-15 miles is the most you should expect to do. Don't attempt more.

WEATHER LORE

The winter camper can't ignore the weather. He has to write weather information into his plans, for while bad weather in summer may be an inconvenience, bad weather in winter can be a killer. You don't need to know all the complicated calculations, but you must get weather information and act upon it.

It is a regrettable fact that while most outdoor people love making lists, and go to great lengths to equip themselves with Food, Clothing, Maps etc., there is rarely a heading that reads 'Weather'. And yet the weather is the one factor that affects all the rest.

PRESSURE

As a general rule, falling pressure indicates the approach of bad weather, while rising pressure indicates good weather. But please note the 'general'. There are few absolutes in weather.

Pressure is measured in bars — and the instrument which measures pressure is called a barometer. In meteorological circles the bar is divided into millibars (mb) and the normal air pressure at sea-level is 1013 millibars; but, we should note that pressure varies, and rises and falls in the pressure from the 1000 mb. mark, are good pointers to the weather. The limits of pressure usually lie between 950 mb. and 1050 mb. Remember that this pressure is *sea-level* pressure. So you need to adjust for height by getting the correct pressure setting for your area by phoning the local Met. Office. Pressure falls about 1 mb for every 30 feet you rise.

On a weather map, points of equal pressure are joined up by lines called isobars. Isobars join points of equal pressure in the same way as contour lines join points of equal height.

TEMPERATURE

Temperature is now expressed in Centigrade (or Celsius) which is a scale based on the melting and boiling points of water. These are 0°C and 100°C respectively.

The other scale still in common use is the Fahrenheit scale. In this the same base is used, but the freezing point is 32°F and the boiling point 212°F. Many people in the U.K. are more familiar with the Fahrenheit scale than with the centigrade scale.

For the outdoor man, camping in the winter, frost and chill need to be reckoned with. Anything below 1°C or 34°F needs to be taken into account in your plans.

The temperature falls, as you rise, by about 3°C every 1000 feet.

HUMIDITY

The atmosphere always contains a certain amount of water vapour, and when this vapour condenses we get different types of weather; especially dew, fog, rain, snow, or the most obvious example, clouds. Fog, hill mist, or fine drizzle, are the result of falling temperatures, or the meeting of cold and warm fronts.

As the temperature falls, air cools, and it can cool until condensation results. This point, the point at which condensation occurs is called the dew point.

WIND

Wind is described in two ways; speed and direction. Wind direction refers to the direction the wind is coming FROM, not going to. So, a wind blowing from Cornwall to Yorkshire is a South-Westerly, not a North-Easterly.

Many parts of the world have 'prevailing winds', that is, the wind blows most often from the same direction. This can be noticed by the effect the prevailing wind has on trees, where they can be seen leaning say, to the North-East in Cornwall, where they have become bent as they grow due to the prevailing South-Westerly winds. Winds are very variable, and can blow at different speeds and directions according to height. High altitude winds can be quite different from winds at sea level.

LOCAL VARIATIONS AND CONDITIONS

There are many ingredients in the weather mix, most notably the effect of local geography, on an overall weather pattern. As a winter camper you must find out all you can about local weather conditions. Ask for information from everyone you meet, and by 'local' we mean where you go camping at weekends as well as where you live.

FORECAST SOURCES

The Press: Most newspapers publish weather forecasts of varyng coverage and use. Some show maps of the U.K. or Europe, and give lots of information. However, you must remember that newspaper information, because it has to be collected, printed, and distributed, is probably at least 12 to 24 hours out of date; and weather conditions can change rapidly. Most 'quality' newspapers have good forecasts.

Television: The television forecasts, especially the 'Late Night' ones on BBC 1, which give forecasts for three days ahead, can be most useful. These forecasts are presented on all T.V. channels, usually close to News time. See the Radio or T.V. Times for details.

Radio Forecasts (Inland): These are on Radio 4 and give outlook forecasts for up to two days ahead. They usually concern inland areas, but this can be useful to coastal yachtsmen. There is a comprehensive 4 minute forecast for land and sea areas on Radio 3 (464m) medium wave, at 6.55 a.m. on weekdays and 7.55 a.m. on Saturdays and Sundays, but check the Radio Times as these times are subject to change. Radio 4 forcasts include regional reports, and details can be found in the Radio Times.

Local Radio Forecasts: The development of local radio stations has been a boon to outdoor people. These stations provide up to the minute local forecasts, often obtained from local as well as national sources, and they take into account local conditions, and up date the information with each broadcast.

You can obtain a booklet giving details of all Weather Advice by writing to the Meteorological Office, Bracknell, Berkshire, England.

Local Knowledge: No list of forecast sources can be complete without local information, and no outdoor man can afford to ignore any local weather advice he can collect from residents and institutions on the spot.

Try and make the source as authoritative as possible. The local airfield tower is a better guide than the landlord's corns, so start there, or the Police Station, the local outdoor shop, and so on. Farmers, fishermen and shepherd are out in all weathers and can give sound advice, so don't neglect to ask for it.

WINTER WINDS

In winter, while the weather generally is worse, the effect of individual winds is quire marked:

Wind Direction	Effect
North	Very cold, rain and snow.
North-East	Very cold, but probably clear.
East	Cold, rain, sleet, snow on high ground.
South-East South	These winds are not common in winter, but clear, cold, brisk days come with these winds.
South-West	Cloudy, drizzle, low cloud and fog, wet.
West	Dull, wet weather.
North-West	Showers, frost, clear spells.

Remember, however, that you must take other information into account, pressure and temperature particularly. Some areas get a lot of shelter from the wind, and are therefore drier and warmer.

Finally, use your eyes and common sense. You can ask people you meet what the latest weather forecast is. The most relevant information you can collect, daily, the better you can plan and the safer and more comfortable you will be. Don't go into the hills in winter if the weather report is unfavourable, and NEVER GO ALONE!

PLANNING A TRIP

If you go up into the hills, watch the weather, but bear in mind the effect of height on temperature, and what this leads to.

If it is raining in the valley it will be sleet at 1000' and a blizzard at 2000. The windward side of a hill may be ten degrees or more colder than the leeward side.

So re-read this chapter, and consider the direct implications of weather, fitness, time and distance IN WINTER, on your camping plans.

Chapter 10

CARE AND MAINTENANCE

Winter can be hard on your gear, though it will suffer less from use than it will from neglect. Even so it will last longer if correctly maintained.

PROOFING

If your tent leaks, it's annoying in summer, but absolutely miserable in winter. In bad weather a small leak will soon get worse. You can buy reproofing preparations in most outdoor shops. You should proof the seams by rubbing them with beeswax or a candle. Temporary proofing agents can also be purchased and it's a good idea to take one with you, in case a drip starts. If the tent gets holed, by a branch or a careless crampon, ring the stockist and get some advice. You can usually obtain patches in similar colours and material, but if the tent is to remain weatherproof, the repair must be expertly done.

DRYING AND MAINTAINING THE TENT

In summer it's a good idea, if you have the time, to leave the tent up for the sun to dry and air. This is rarely possible in winter, so you arrive home with a wet tent, which must then be dried.

What we do is to drape it over the kitchen table overnight. This dries it off, and with the guys attached to dressers and fridge, it airs as well.

Before you dry it, sluice off any mud, but *do not* use any detergents on hard spots. Just water. Most mud can be brushed off, but unless your tent is kept clean the grit will eat into the fibres and cause wear. A nozzle on the vacuum cleaner will get the grit out from a fitted ground-sheet.

Check guys for wear and seams for snapped stitches. Have spare rubber guys, as they soon perish. Rub all tent pegs down with a lightly oiled cloth and straighten any which are bent. The zips can be eased by rubbing with pencil lead (graphite), but NOT with oil.

SLEEPING BAGS AND MATS

Dry the bags out gently, then hang up in the wardrobe. Don't roll them up if you can help it. If you have a damp down bag, keep shaking it gently to loosen and loft the feathers. Dry the mats thoroughly before stowing.

STOVES AND COOKSETS
Clean off mud and moisture and wipe dry. Beware of rust. Make sure that no food in packets or tins is leaking.

TORCHES
Remove the batteries and dry out the insides so that they are free from damp.

CLOTHES AND BOOTS
Dry and brush off any mud. Clean out the soles of Vibram boots, and wash them clean. A coat of polish or a smear of dubbin may be called for.

RUCKSACKS
Rucksacks get a lot of hammering in winter. Be sure no water or ice has melted in the pockets, or the main compartment, and hang it upside-down to drain.

WATERPROOFS
The rubbing of rucksacks may wear away the proofing on your shell clothing. Check at the shoulders and waist, and apply a recommended proofing agent if you see signs of wear.

The rule for care and maintenance of gear is that you carry it out just *after* the trip and not just *before*.

Have a cup of tea when you get back, but before you have a bath and collapse before the box, have all your gear sorted out, and drying nicely with a list of repairs (if any) to do when all is dry.

Then, these done, with your gear all ready, you can start looking out of the window, listening to the weather forecasts, and wonder where to go next.

And good luck to you wherever it is!